The Healing Coloring Book
of Lady Lotus Blossom

Lon Mansaray

BALBOA
PRESS

A DIVISION OF HAY HOUSE

Balboa Press books may be ordered through booksellers or by contacting:

Balboa Press
A Division of Hay House
1663 Liberty Drive
Bloomington, IN 47403
www.balboapress.com
1 (877) 407-4847

Because of the dynamic nature of the Internet, any web addresses or links contained in
this book may have changed since publication and may no longer be valid. The views
expressed in this work are solely those of the author and do not necessarily reflect the views
of the publisher, and the publisher hereby disclaims any responsibility for them.

The author of this book does not dispense medical advice or prescribe the use of any technique as a form of
treatment for physical, emotional, or medical problems without the advice of a physician, either directly or
indirectly. The intent of the author is only to offer information of a general nature to help you in your quest
for emotional and spiritual well-being. In the event you use any of the information in this book for yourself,
which is your constitutional right, the author and the publisher assume no responsibility for your actions.

Any people depicted in stock imagery provided by Thinkstock are models,
and such images are being used for illustrative purposes only.
Certain stock imagery © Thinkstock.

ISBN: 978-1-5043-3364-1 (sc)
ISBN: 978-1-5043-3365-8 (e)

Library of Congress Control Number: 2015908869

Print information available on the last page.

Balboa Press rev. date: 09/28/2015

Contents

The Healing Coloring book
of Lady Lotus Blossom

This coloring book belongs to _____

_____

Instructions to enter the Wonderful World of Lady Lotus Blossom

Before coloring each page follow these instructions:

Close your eyes and take a deep breath. Relax and imagine a beautiful butterfly.

Gently place your hands on the coloring book and keep them there until they feel warm.

Now repeat after me:

"I now allow my heart and my hands to dance the dance of color energy!

I now embrace this special place that lives inside of me.

Here I go

...take a leap

Faith is where I'll land

All is good, all is great

And I am WHOLE AGAIN."

Enter....

Madam Butterfly

How curious to find a butterfly that can't fly

All beautiful, colorful and delicate.

Wounded. But still alive with so much courage in every attempt to fly.

Hello Madam Butterfly! Are you ok? Hop on my finger and I'll carry you away.

Madam butterfly smiled at me, she said, "Put me down! The only way I get
strong is to appreciate the ground. I'm thankful I am walking. Might not
be able to fly but I'm happy to be breathing. Yes, Lady Lotus, I'm alive."

BE GRATEFUL FOR EVERY MOMENT...ALL MOMENTS COUNT...

 # Mr. Sunflower

Running through a maze of sunflowers, I crossed the path of its seeds.
There was a sunflower. Bent over. Looked like he was on his knees.

"Mr. Sunflower, what are you doing?"

"Giving back," he said in a rush. "If we always take we will
have too much, and nothing will ever be enough."

TAKE ONE DAY AT A TIME. GIVE IT YOUR VERY BEST.

Swap Swan

It's one bird I know that doesn't like the mirror

Always at the back of the line or trying to hide, I figure.

"Swap Swan, would you look a little deeper?

So much beauty and all that grace, open your eyes to see!

There are no flaws in all creation

We are all one in the same.

Beautiful...

...each one a different name."

YOU ARE LOVE ...AND YOUR LOVE... IS BEAUTIFUL.

KINGDOM OF ALL

I, Lady Lotus Blossom visited a place called the Kingdom of All. As far as the eye could see I saw people in many different colors, shapes and sizes. They were kind, loving and peaceful. Not one of them were mean, unloving or angry. Holding hands, they prayed, gave thanks and forgave. None were sick, ill or diseased among them.

WE CREATE OUR WORLD. ALL...or Nothing at ALL.

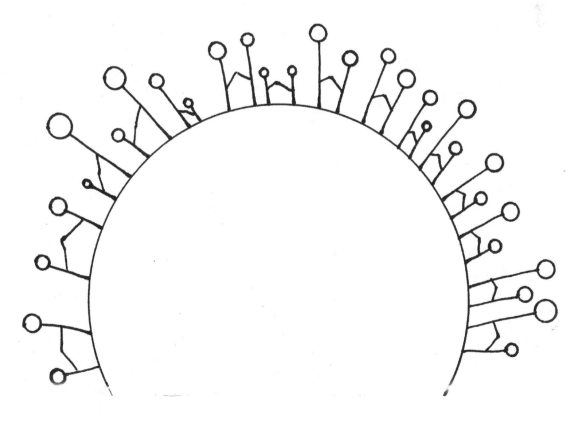

She Blooms

While sitting at a picnic table under a shade tree, a little voice called out to me. So I answered, not seeing a face or a person. I was being watched by a bloomer and its curiosity couldn't be quenched. I was tickled to meet the acquaintance of a flower fairy called Bloom. I promised to close my eyes, but couldn't. I snuck a peek. Oops! She caught me! And in a ball of Golden dust, she hopped away.

No moment that you are meant to have will be missed.

The Journey on Saint Lamanz

I, Lady Lotus Blossom, was asked to go on a journey aboard the Saint Lamanz Fare Train. This trip was like none I had ever been on in all my travels. The journey had lots of steep hills and drops. I saw beautiful valleys and lakes. I heard music playing from heaven itself. High in the mountains, the train went up, up and back down again. Though the ride was bumpy, it was beautiful nonetheless. And while I had to get off, the scenery I'll never forget.

The scenery in every moment is worth a pause on the journey.

Sir Charles's Bell

Once I had the honor of serving the Honorable Sir Charles while he was under the weather. To serve him better I gave him a bell to ring when he needed anything. After several rings I thought that he had everything he needed to be comfortable and to get some rest...

To my surprise the ringing didn't stop.

Sometimes your presence is all that's needed.

Be Present.

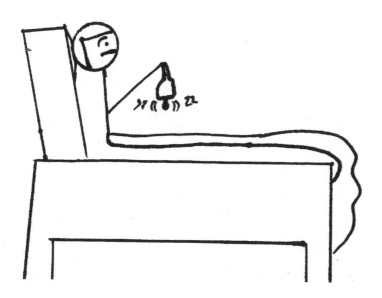

Silly Zim, The Hatter

Silly Zim, you and that hat of laughter got me in stitches. A frown upside down is a great smile. A little laughter dries up tears and a big hug comforts away the fears.

Silly Zim, let me be...I'm laughing so hard I've got to wee!

When you're laughing, *it kills fear.*

Weavers

I saw a vision into the heavens, a room with straw in it; and many hands weaving the straw into big baskets. Each piece of straw had a prayer request on it and they were all on a big table. Now, it was amazing to see those hands go to the table and place different prayers in different piles. In each pile all the prayers that were placed were somehow linked. Another set of hands started weaving these prayer straws together. I didn't understand why the prayers were being weaved together, but after a short period of time, a big basket was created. We send up prayers and heaven gives us baskets to receive.

Each prayer becomes an opportunity to receive.

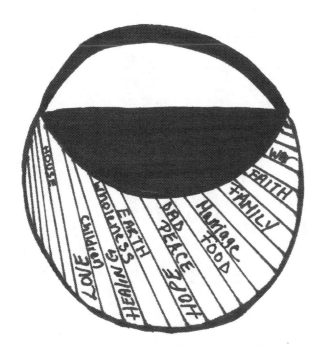

SonZu, Hand of Fire

How could I forget my friend SonZu? He had a broken heart and didn't know what to do. So much fire he would burn out. Then holler and scream and want to fight. Though he was wise, his heart was broke...I still remember how he used to smoke. Those hands burst into flames. I touched his heart and called his name. He calmed down and looked at me. Meanwhile, that broken heart healed up fast. And ole SonZu finally let go of the past.

Let your fire be fueled by the Love of God that lives inside. Real love cures a broken Heart.

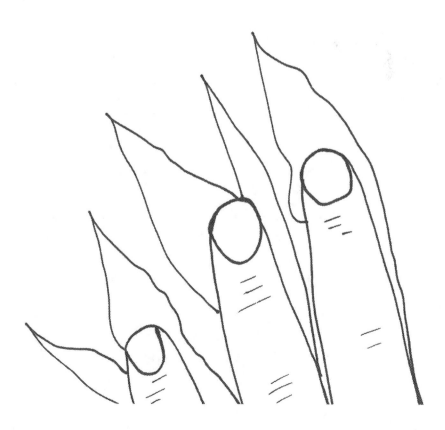

Molly Polly

This little lady is just so cute

Watch so much TV and too many cartoons to boot.

She loves to skip, hop, jump and play.

She loves to sing and boy she can pray.

Her mind is filled with so much to create.

Just watch her dance and celebrate!

Celebrate your dreams and visions before they happen.

WATCHING OVER ME

This is coming straight from my heart. I have seen so much in such a short while. With all my amazing stories I can tell you one thing I know for sure... I am safe. Watching over me is a security system that doesn't fail. I don't call it luck, instead, I think love perhaps fits best. We are so loved that things just don't happen by chance. We are ever-guided on this journey and never alone to face our fears if we just believe.

Our Father is watching over us.

Zim's Princess Lolah

I find myself being drawn back to my friend Zim the Hatter. As much as he made me laugh there was a time that his smile vanished and even though he laughed, it was in pain. You see, Zim was blessed with a princess. The Queen decided to move far away and took the princess to a distant land. Zim tried so hard to convince her to stay, but in all of his loving gestures, the queen's mind was made up. Zim missed the little Princess. Lolah was her name and her beautiful spirit lifted everyone around her. She was the apple of her father's eye. Lolah loved her pinks, pocketbooks and high heels. Lolah was quite the actress. No matter how far away she was, oh how she loved Zim. The queen went on to have other children and Lolah had her father's hat of laughter. She kept her siblings in line and helped the queen all she could. Finally, after some years, Zim and Lolah were back in the same land. Zim found his smile again. I can see them both sitting in the grass with those hats on laughing. That laughter is contagious. Even the animals look like, "what is going on?" The curious thing is... after you color the next picture you're going to laugh and laugh! It's good medicine after all!

May you laugh without pain or sorrow knowing that everything
you thought you lost is restored in a moment...this very one.

The Beholder

I visited the country where the air was clean and crisp and the June bugs were just as green as grass. Sitting on my Grandma's blanket I became the Beholder. My eyes were looking up, down and all around. Taking in the smells and the sounds. To behold so much beauty in just one day was like a lifetime to a child who loves to play. Butterflies chasing and grass tickling my feet. The sun was blushing with all that heat. My sis got on granny's clothes with her red fox. I got on granny's heels with some knee-high socks.

BEHOLD! YOUR GREATEST MOMENTS ARE HERE.

The Way

Sometimes people come into your life to show you the way. This coming was unannounced and unexpected. Nevertheless, I was open to receive more than I could take in at once. Gentle, loving, kind and so peaceful is the way that was chosen for me. Everything was prepared, all I had to do was receive. This new way of seeing, thinking and feeling was absolutely what I was waiting for.

You will have what you need along the way.

Speaking to Genes

In this moment I choose to speak to Genes.

"Deep down within I call you forth!

I speak this unto you! "You shall be quick to repair!
You shall cut off at the root, all disease!

All despair! You will cease to reboot!

You repairers, get to work and make no delay!

Along this path, along this strain of broken DNA.

His blood, your blood, one in the same...

All infirmity be removed.

I am Whole. I am Healed

as Jesus Christ

Proclaimed."

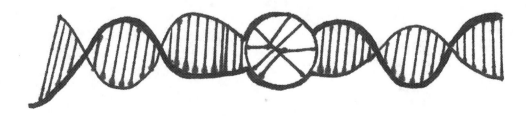

Looking up

I look up a lot to see what the sky is saying to me.

The sky speaks loud, a message that we must listen to.

It gives us so much beauty that goes unnoticed.

I lifted my head until my neck touched my back.

I stretch and embrace the beauty of just being open.

The Creator of All formed us in His image. Anything is possible. Just believe.

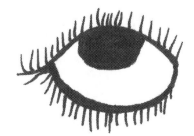 

34

Lee-Lee's Praise

Oh little Lee-Lee, who wiped your smile away?

"I've given them mercy," she said. "They can't take away my Praise.

It's hard to find that first smile after you've been broken.

Like a caterpillar to a butterfly, I have praised my way through!

No matter what anyone has done

God, I'm always trusting in You.

So I sing, drum and praise

'Cause, my smile is here in my heart and that is where it will stay!"

Only allow your smile to leave your face... Not your heart.

They Love

Love is never broken

No matter how hard it gets

It sticks in there with you

For you, I'll never quit

Yes, a lot has happened

Our plight has had a shift

So let's just hold on to each other

Until all our pieces fit

Unconditional love surpasses patience.

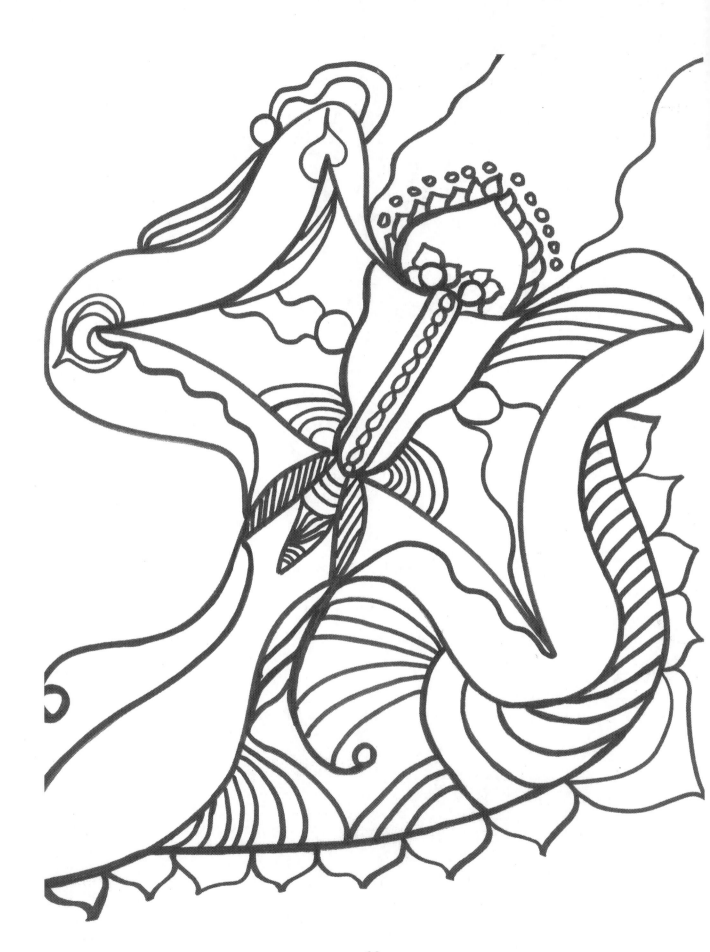

The Dance of Cha-Chew

Dance! Dance! Dance!

Cha, Cha, Chew

Bouncy, Bouncy, Bouncy

Boo, Boo, Boom

Come on now, shake it!

Cha, Cha, Chew

Move those legs

Boo, Boo, Boom

Joyous movement blesses us with strength.

Don't Mind Michael

My buddy Michael is such a big help. Don't mind him, though, he said what he meant. Very straightforward, he speaks his truth with some high notes that just might take off the roof. He loves his family and will do all he can. We all love Michael; he's such a great man.

Our words should only be truth…And that truth is powerful!

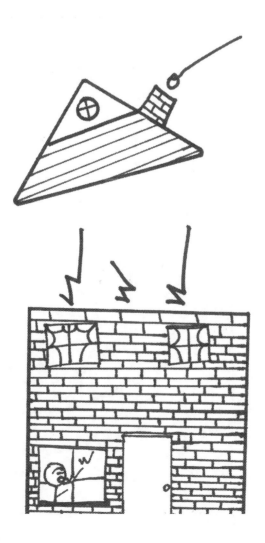

The Carpet Sign

It was a mid-summer's evening and I had friends over enjoying the ambience in my living room. The air was lightly scented with candles and angelic music played off in the distance. I had very plush pink carpet. One friend decided to lay on my carpet. The rest of us, we sat quietly on couches. A peace that surpasses all understanding filled the room with sweet silence. My friend that was lying on the floor suddenly called out for help. I rushed over to see if he was ok. With tears streaming down his face he said, "I can't get up". I comforted him and told him all was well. He began to relax and several minutes later he was able to get up. We looked amazed as he began to describe a loving presence he felt cover him like an invisible hug. The night continued and my guests got up to leave. I went back to the living room to get my friend's keys. I looked down and all I could do was stare. In the exact place where he had laid was the imprint of an angel's face and wings. I called everyone to witness this sight. We were all amazed. After that night, as long as I worked in the living room the carpet continued to create beautiful signs of God's Love.

God's special love is found in signs all around us.

Love

Not Alone

I AM Here with you

A New Son

We all experience painful situations in different ways, but pain is still pain all the same. Change is a pain in itself if you allow it to be. Nothing stays the same for too long. The wind of change blows through us and we must all surrender to it. Change is sometimes viewed as a means for loss and confusion, or associated with something unbearable or heartache. Especially when we've lost someone we love. That change can be so severe because death is so fictionally final. But it's never really over. We are and will always be like our Creator. We sometimes hold on when others have to leave to be present in their own life without us. We are crutches for one another sometimes. Looking for someone to love while we neglect loving ourselves. We void ourselves of so many moments waiting for someone to enjoy them with us. We hold on selfishly when it's time to surrender and accept. In doing this, we deny our eyes the enjoyment of so much that life has to offer. It's never really over. Death is a fictional presentation of a fact that doesn't exist. When death comes in any form, we shall be born again. Unless a man be born again, he cannot see the Kingdom of God within himself.

He who sees the son becomes anew.

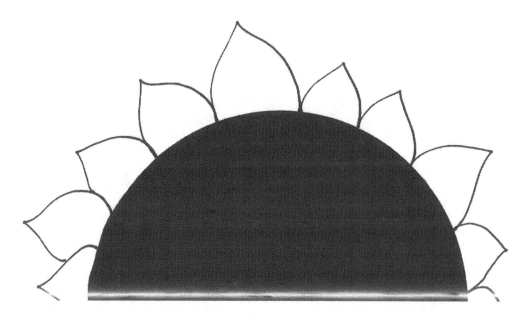

6 Plus 1

We are six plus one light shining bright in heaven

Our life has been anything but normal

Having little, we have gained so much

3 darlings dressed in pink

3 dressed in suits and ties

1 light of us prayed for us in heaven

All of us from one

We are all different, but all the same

And all carry the same last name

Family is where we learn community.

Community is where we realize we are all

One.

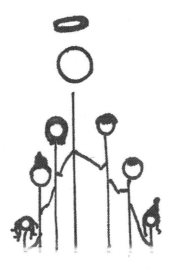

Shemahme the Sacred Matriarch

I am an observer of the beauty of nature. A love for what is pure and innocent lead me to discover the secrets of Shemahme. Shemahme was outcast from her fellow tribe at an early age. At times she was deprived of the love, tenderness and warmth of a mother's nurturing hand to grab her when she was scared the most. Shemahme was closed off to this most natural love. When she gave birth to her daughter she wondered, how she could give what wasn't given to her? Frightened and not having the guidance of the elders, Shemahme had to learn to love this child she couldn't understand. That baby girl would run off and Shemahme would be so angry at all the trouble this now young female would give her. Baby after baby Shemahme learned how to hug and nurture. Now that first born baby girl never left her heart even though now she is a grown woman. Persistent to mother, nurture and love her, Shemahme made every effort to create a bond with the one that slipped away not knowing how to love as she did not. No matter how far her daughter would run away Shemahme would call out for her so she could always find her way back safely in her mommy's arms. I, Lady Lotus Blossom, learned we have to heal our pass. No matter how old we get, we are still healing from our past. Shemahme teaches us that the position of matriarch is unconditional love, faith, security and communication.

May the love and nurturing of a praying mother find you now
on your journey and lead you back safely into love.

The two dresses of Mary Jane Granmi

Now I told you about Shemahme, but the root of her trouble started way back when. We hurt because of the generational issues that get passed down to us to be healed. Our lives can be full of dancing and celebration and all of a sudden our innocence is snatched away like your breath when you get punched in the stomach really hard. I was told this story. From all the passed down knowledge I have received, none has caused my heart to carry such a diligence to heal my own life and spread the message of wholeness to all I meet like this one.

Little Mary Jane was sitting on the back porch about to leave her family. She was full of a shame that was never hers to carry. In her suitcase were two dresses. The only real dresses she owned. Prior to this, at the tender age of 13, she lost her innocence to a predator that climbed through her window. Mary Jane's eyes were so full of water now in her 80's as she bared her soul to me. The naked truth. Both of her parents died and never heard. She said, "I was assaulted and I didn't want my parents to retaliate so I told no one". "My mother told me to come in the house; that they loved me regardless. I was just looked upon as fast or promiscuous. When those doctors told me I was pregnant I screamed, 'what is in me?!' I sat there in absolute shock," she said as she stared directly into my eyes. Mary Jane is one sibling out of a very large family. I wondered, how can one live with such a secret. But this is Mary Jane we are talking about. She managed to carry 19 babies in her womb, 13 of which survived. More pain added, and still she raised her children to cook, clean and live God-fearing lives. I laid in bed with her as she spoke of things she had been through in her life. I began rubbing her white hair and realizing that this is real strength and resilience. I started singing as tears rolled down both of our eyes. This was generational healing.

We wait so long to tell the story that will set us free from pain. We wonder why our heart gives out and our limbs ache. It is only a symptom of our spirit crying out to be healed. In spite of it all, she has endured and she has taught me to live. To have strength and do my best with what I'm given. I am open to tell my truth, my story so others can be free. No matter what life gives you or how bad your story may be, know that your life has purpose.

 **Even After Reality There's Hope**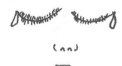

Re-Birth Day

I had lived to see another year. What should have been a happy occasion was met with the illusion that I was forgotten and unloved by others. I still remember that day. It was cold and started to snow. I felt an urge to just go outside and walk. It was as if I were being lead to a particular place wherever that may have been. As I walked, I started feeling the presence of God around me in a tangible way. So much that, for a moment, I stopped and looked around. Now I, Lady Lotus Blossom tell these stores, which are pure truths. This isn't some fantasy or fiction. Right down in that snow were four footprints instead of two.

No, this isn't the story of the man being carried! Curious, right? I was stuck, my eyes told no lie. All at once, my heart seemed to open and tears streamed down my eyes like crystals bending the light from the hiding sun. I lifted my hands and took a deep breath. I am not alone! God walks with me on snow-covered roads. Ha! You will have to wait for more of this story, this is one of my greatest adventures yet. I will say that God arrives when you're ready to meet him.

One isn't alone. It is a whole lot of things together. You're never alone.

OUR TRUTH

This is our truth.

We come from not much, but all. Many battles tried hard to put out the light.

This is our truth.

Many we love had no love and watched our fight.

This is our truth.

We were handed laughter in exchange for our
tears. Gifts in exchange for our fears.

This is our Truth.

Many have joined our tribe. Many we have loved, cared for and taken in.

Giving much out from what God has given.

THIS IS OUR TRUTH.

We have not talked love, we have walked it.

This is our truth.

We have not given up but fought the good fight of faith.

We stand united.

This is our Truth.

We come from not much, but all. Many battles tried hard to put out the light.

This is our truth.

Actions make words genuine ...this is truth.

RELEASE

In all that I am I now release

Sorrow, pain and anger, be released

Hatred, guilt, grief and shame

Be released

All hurt, harm and blame

Be released

I choose to release and let this energy go

No more room to store

Can't hold it no more

And with this, I close the door

I RELEASE

You become what's in you. RELEASE...

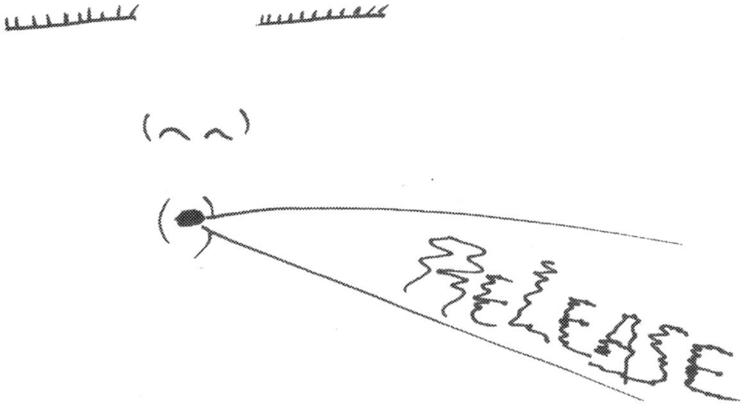

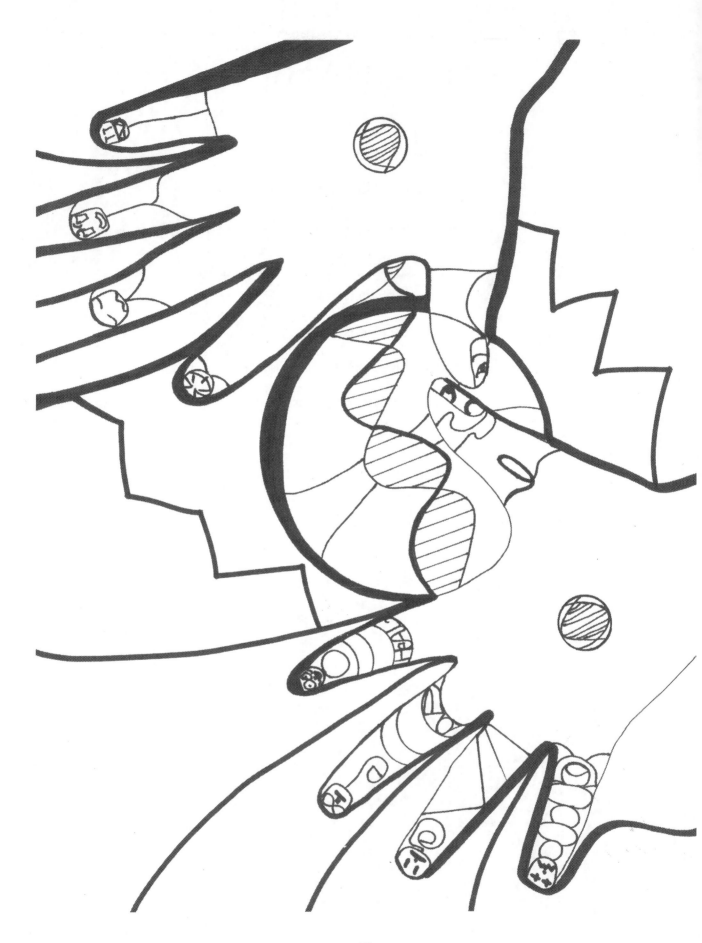

Reprogram

Here is the new pattern to use. Simply read aloud and turn the page.
Place your hand over the hands on the page and then color.

I am restored by this love

No sin against myself

I operate in this love

I give it to myself

I am love

I am that

The reflection of my Creator

We are made in the image of infinite Love. *I am love in action.*

THE STRENGTH OF RAHSHE

Never have I seen the strength of a woman like I witnessed in Rahshe. Rahshe is limber, fast and strong. She is disciplined and well-learned in her curriculum. I suppose it was because she read the dictionary for hours in the closet while sucking on bread. That was Rahshe's favorite. The wisdom she walked in at a young age caused her to develop a very unique strength. I don't know anyone that she couldn't make smile. Rahshe could make the worst days so fun. We would play dress up and I would push her around in our cabinet car. Rahshe taught me so much about myself. She made me promise I would never leave her. I tried but couldn't keep that promise. Rahshe finally forgave me in the end. I have reaped what I have sown, now she has moved away. I still can see her making me laugh until I cry. Rahshe has always had the strength of the wind, a mighty force to be reckoned with, but also the gentleness of a summer breeze that doesn't move the leaves on a tree much. When I think I can't, she stirs the strength within me. "No excuses, don't give up, you can do it". And then she would make me laugh! I am the oldest, but she is Rahshe, my big sister in strength.

Unconditional love is strength when given to the weak at heart.

Nibby New Shoes

Put that smile back on your face

Those new shoes are walking to a brand new place

You can do it! Oh, yes you can!

You are mommy and daddy's

Big little man

Such a good helper and big brother, too

Just keep on praying and see what God can do!

I see it clear. I see it plain.

He will bring your family together again.

No matter how hard the situation, God will answer your prayer.

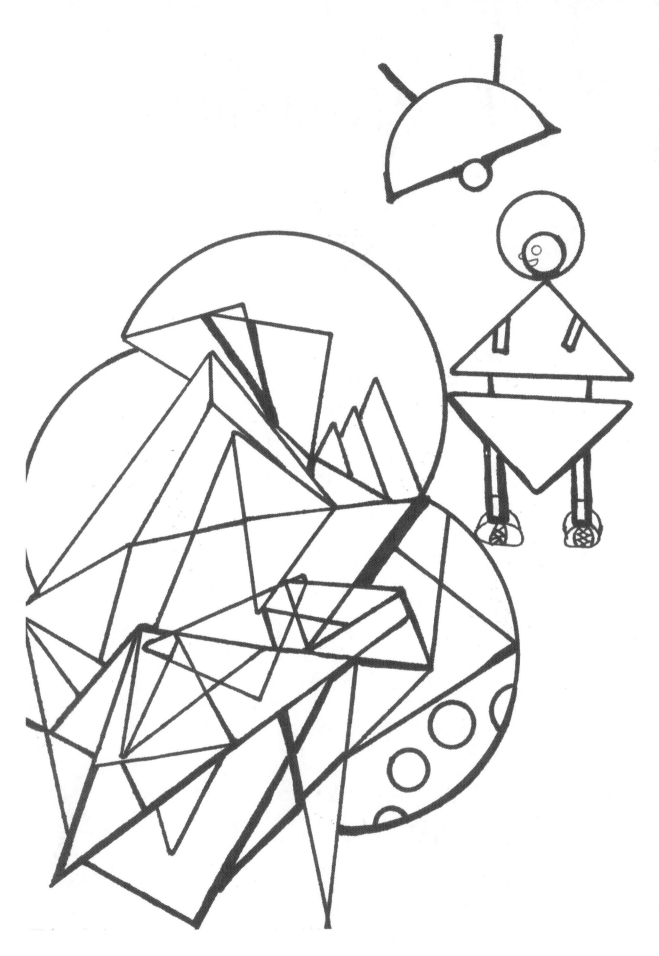

Lady Lotus Blossom's Re-birth

Back to my birthday story...

I continued to walk and then all at once I started speaking out loud to an invisible, but very tangible force... the Almighty God. This was real. It was liberating. The response was simple.

"STOP!"

Immediately, I stopped. Happy Birthday rang out from inside of me, but it wasn't me... "Turn around!" rang out second.

I paused in amazement, realizing that I was standing at the corner facing the park. As instructed, I turned slowly and I noticed that snow had begun to fall on a pine tree now facing me. That pine tree had grown around and intertwined with a rose bush. Nestled among the pine needles was one single pink baby rose that was in bloom. Needless to say it was the best birthday gift I have ever received. I now understand why Jesus wept. When I felt lost, forgotten, unloved and down, God chose that moment on the day of my birth to change my life forever for the better.

In this moment I declare you shall have a tangible moment with the Almighty God that will change your life forever.

HANDY HENRY

Oh handy Henry! Had to grow up fast and be so responsible it was such a task. "I have got to shovel snow to help my mom," he would say. Go grab his brother and they would shovel away. He would cut that grass and buy his family a meal, taking up the slack while his dad was ill. Henry was handy, he could turn a buck quick to keep his family going when his dad was most sick. Henry never smiled. I guess he was just a little tired and just a little sad because ever since he was young he was a little dad. I pray for Henry to this very day that God would wipe his frown away. Over the years Henry quit being a dad and started worrying more about all he never had. With two children of his own he forgot how to play like he used to with Lee and Michael all day. Henry is a great dad that was self-taught. Only if he could remember that's his special part.

If we only focus on the bad, how can we see our good?

Changing Focus

Boomy Loom

(Boo-Mee-Loom)

Wide-eyed, Ms. Boomy Loom is not from here many may say. Her face could light up a dark room like the sun. She is free-loving, innocent and pure at her core. So much repaired brokenness in those eyes you can get lost in. If there is one word to describe her life it is "Wholeness". To be whole is to take in each broken piece you are given and own it. It is what makes you who you are. Our story is only perfect when the imperfections are viewed as defining character in our picture called self. Never be afraid or ashamed of who you are. There is purpose even when we don't understand. Boomy Loom loved to dance to Bertha Butt Boogie. She could swing her thighs before she could walk. She is louder than life and more loving than a lot of people can even see. If she could heal every broken person, she would. Boomy Loom could never stand to see the suffering of others. Her compassion stretches her ability to use sound judgment sometimes, however, **she is brave enough to tell her story in the sequel to this book.**

Wholeness is a work in progress as our story continues...Keep creating.

You

Thank you for traveling on this journey with me. Through each page, I hope you have been inspired to be the change of love this world needs. If you are ill, I send prayers for your healing. If you are broken, I pray that you come to wholeness. If you are without love, I pray you hug and love yourself. God is love and we are made in this image.

I love you All ♥

Lady Lotus Blossom

Acknowledgements

With great honor, appreciation and gratitude I thank my husband Bryan Mansaray, for supporting this vision and loving me as Christ loves us unconditionally, honey I love you. Juan and Jasmyn I love you and thank you for opening your arms and receiving me to be a part of your life. To my parents, Charles and Jeanne Galloway, all that I am belongs to you both. I love you. To my loving grandparents, Henry and Lenora Palmer, Charles and Gladys Galloway, thank you for your prayers and the experiences you have passed down as wisdom. To my siblings, Rachelle, Charles, Thomas, Deborah and Zachary, I love you all so very much. May this book inspire each of you to keep reaching for better and encourage you to never give up. To my nieces, Nala, Kaylia, Zachia, and my nephew, Charles, auntie loves you! Never forget the lessons in this book. To all my aunts and uncles, thank you! I love you all. To my Goddaughter, Diamond, I love you. Keep pressing forward fearlessly. To my mentor, Mrs.Suchinta, thank you for teaching the way to wholeness. Hay House and Balboa Press, thank you for the publishing opportunity. To Shannon Vanessa Webster, may God bless every writing that you pen. Much love and appreciation for all your wonderful editing and writing skills. Phil Bailey,thank you for believing in my vision and capturing the images on this book. To Bryan Mansaray, Overseer and Apostle Galloway, Barbara Wilder, Nikkitta Jones, Daria Thompson and Crysta Pangburn, your investments towards my vision are priceless. God Bless you! To my spiritual parents and close friends, I love you. Never give up. To my church family, I love you all. This coloring book is proof that God is Faithful. To all my friends who have supported my vision over the years, thank you, I love you and may God Bless us ALL!

Your Dreams and Prayers Here

WHAT IS YOUR STORY

_____

_____

_____

_____

_____

_____

_____

_____

_____

_____

_____

_____

IF YOU WOULD LIKE TO EMAIL LADY LOTUS BLOSSOM YOUR STORY CONTACT US @

ladylotuscoloringbook@gmail.com

Printed in the United States
By Bookmasters